A Fun Run

Teaching Tips

Yellow Level 3

This book focuses on the phoneme /qu/.

Before Reading
- Discuss the title. Ask readers what they think the book will be about.
- Sound out the words on page 3 together.

Read the Book
- Ask readers to use a finger to follow along with each word as it is read.
- Encourage readers to break down unfamiliar words into units of sound. Then, ask them to string the sounds together to create the words.
- Urge readers to point out when the focused phonics phoneme appears in the text.

After Reading
- Encourage children to reread the book independently or with a friend.
- Ask simple questions about the text to check for understanding. Have them find the pages that have the answers to your questions.

© 2024 Booklife Publishing
This edition is published by arrangement with Booklife Publishing.

North American adaptations © 2024 Jump!
5357 Penn Avenue South
Minneapolis, MN 55419
www.jumplibrary.com

Decodables by Jump! are published by Jump! Library.
All rights reserved. No part of this book may be reproduced in any form without written permission from the publisher.

Library of Congress Cataloging-in-Publication Data is available at www.loc.gov or upon request from the publisher.

ISBN: 979-8-88996-807-8 (hardcover)
ISBN: 979-8-88996-808-5 (paperback)
ISBN: 979-8-88996-809-2 (ebook)

Photo Credits

Images are courtesy of Shutterstock.com. With thanks to Getty Images, Thinkstock Photo and iStockphoto. Cover – hanapon1002, Mega Pixel. 4–5 – PETROS PAPAPETROPOULOS, lakeemotion. 6–7 – Shane White, Sura Nualpradid. 8–9 – FCG, sportpoint, WoodysPhotos. 10–11 – rblfmr, EvrenKalinbacak. 14–15 – Shutterstock.

Can you find these words in the book?

quick

quit

quite

This is a fun run. The runners all run.

Runners

They are quick. Are they as quick as the dog?

Runners can get quite hot in the sun.

He needs a hat.

They get a quick sip.

They need to run quick to keep up.

They are not as quick up the hill.

They will not quit now.

They did not quit!

Can you say this sound and draw it with your finger?

Trace the letters /qu/ to complete each word. Say the words out loud.

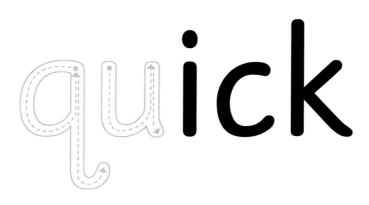ick

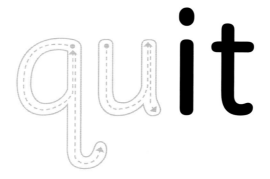it

ite

What other words can you spell with /qu/?

___iz   ___een

___ill

 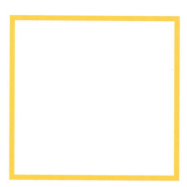

___ail   s___are

___arter

Practice reading the book again:

This is a fun run. The runners all run.

They are quick. Are they as quick as the dog?

Runners can get quite hot in the sun.

He needs a hat.

They get a quick sip.

They need to run quick to keep up.

They are not as quick up the hill.

They will not quit now.

They did not quit!